IT WORKS!
Revolution in
Transportation

John Perritano

Marshall Cavendish
Benchmark
New York

This edition first published in 2010 in the United States
of America by Marshall Cavendish Benchmark.

Marshall Cavendish Benchmark
99 White Plains Road
Tarrytown, NY 10591
www.marshallcavendish.us

Library of Congress Cataloging-in-Publication Data

Perritano, John.
Revolution in transportation / by John Perritano.
p. cm. — (It works!)
Summary: "Discusses the history of transportation, how the technology was developed,
and the science behind it"—Provided by publisher.
Includes bibliographical references and index.
ISBN 978-0-7614-4379-7
1. Transportation engineering—Juvenile
literature. I. Title.
TA1149.P47 2010
629.0409–dc22
2008054366

Cover: Q2AMedia Art Bank
Half Title: Shutterstock.
P7: Karl R. Martin/Shutterstock; P7(inset)tr: Kimberly; P7(inset)cr: Ivan Cholakov/Shutterstock;
P11tl: Lars Christensen/Shutterstock; P11tr: Icholakov/Dreamstime; P11b: Hideo Kurihara/
Alamy; P15: Lisa Marie Saiki zero motorcycles; P15(inset): Cracknell/Shutterstock;
P19: Hulton Archive/Getty Images; P23: Bigstockphoto; P27: Mike Massee/XCOR.
Illustrations: Q2AMedia Art Bank

Created by Q2AMedia
Series Editor: Jessica Cohn
Art Director: Sumit Charles
Client Service Manager: Santosh Vasudevan
Project Manager: Shekhar Kapur
Designer: Shilpi Sarkar
Illustrators: Aadil Ahmed, Rishi Bhardwaj,
Kusum Kala, Parwinder Singh and Sanyogita Lal
Photo research: Sakshi Saluja

Printed in Malaysia

135642

Contents

Up, Up, and Away!

J oseph and Etienne Montgolfier grew up in France during the 1700s. People traveled by horse, carriage, mule, and boat back then. The brothers thought that there must be a better way to get around. They wondered what it would be like to rise above the clouds.

The brothers tried to make paper float. Then, they discovered that heated air made a balloon rise from the ground. On September 19, 1783, the brothers showed off their hot-air balloon to the king and queen of France. The balloon's passengers that day were a sheep, a duck, and a rooster. The balloon floated for eight minutes. It landed about 2 miles (3 kilometers) away.

Two months later, two brave men climbed aboard a Montgolfier balloon and drifted over Paris for about 5.5 miles (9 km). It was the start of the age of flight.

Meet the Montgolfiers

Joseph and Etienne Montgolfier were the sons of a rich papermaker. Joseph, born in 1740, was the elder. Etienne was born in 1745. There were sixteen children in their family in all. Joseph was called a dreamer. Etienne was a natural in business. The brothers **experimented** many times as they tried to make their balloon float. At first, they thought that dense, or very thick, smoke lifted the balloon. They then realized that hot air gave their invention the **lift** it needed.

We were thinking there was a special gas inside our balloon. Our thought was wrong. Yet, we were headed in the right direction.

What is really happening here? Hot air is rising in cooler air. Why? Hot air has less mass per unit of volume. Mass measures the force that holds something down on the ground. Volume measures the space something takes up.

Hot air, not a special gas, makes the balloon rise. Hot air weighs less than air that is cooler.

A Trash Bag Balloon

toaster

empty cereal box

kitchen trash bag
with no ties

adult helper

1 Fashion a large tube out of the cereal box. Push in the corners. Tuck in the flaps on both ends of the box.

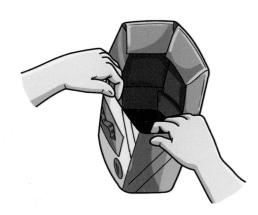

2 Place the tube over the openings of a toaster.

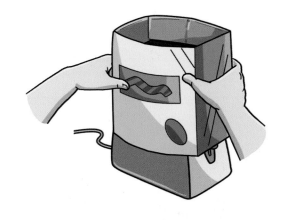

3 With an adult's help, put the trash bag over the tube. Make sure the bag covers both the tube and the toaster.

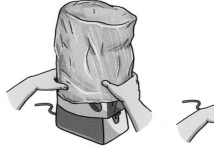

4 Turn on the toaster. Watch as the trash bag fills with hot air and takes off. You might try the experiment again in a room with a taller ceiling. See how hot air gives your balloon a rise!

WHO WOULD HAVE THOUGHT?

Hot Airships

Airships, or blimps, are like hot-air balloons. They rely on gas that is lighter than air to create lift. Unlike hot-air balloons, though, airships can move by their own power. They can hang overhead for hours. They can even cross the ocean.

Airships were used as bombers during World War I (1914–1918). After the war, passengers boarded airships and flew across the Atlantic Ocean. Airships, however, were big. They were also hard to steer. They were dangerous in other ways, too. Lightning or an electrical spark could set them on fire. Wild winds could damage them.

The days of passenger airship service ended in 1937. That's when the German-built *Hindenburg* blew up in Lakehurst, New Jersey. It was filled with **hydrogen** gas. Today's blimps mainly use **helium**. Helium does not burn as fast as hydrogen does.

Modern blimps are often used for advertising.

The Wright Way

In the early 1900s, no one had flown in an aircraft with a motor. Wilbur and Orville Wright believed they could be the first. "From the time we were little children, my brother Orville and myself lived together, played together, worked together, and in fact, thought together," Wilbur Wright once said.

The brothers worked in a bicycle shop in Dayton, Ohio. The shop gave them a living, but it was the possibility of flying that thrilled the Wrights. They read everything they could about the new field of **aeronautics**. They then began building **gliders**. The Wright brothers worked out problems of balance, lift, and control.

History happened one morning on the windy island of Kitty Hawk, South Carolina. The date was December 17, 1903. The Wright brothers succeeded in flying the first gasoline-powered aircraft. That first flight lasted twelve seconds. Now the airplane is a common sight in the sky.

Meet the Wrights

Wilbur Wright was born in 1867. He was the third son of Milton and Susan Wright. His brother Orville was born in 1871. In 1889, the two brothers began a business together. They started a four-page weekly newspaper. Then they opened a bicycle repair shop in Dayton, Ohio. Their biggest shared project, however, was the airplane. In 1903, the *Wright Flyer* took off. Orville was at the controls. Orville sent his father a telegraph from Kitty Hawk that day: *"Success . . . four flights . . . longest 57 seconds . . . inform press . . . home Christmas."*

When we were kids, our father brought us a toy that worked like a helicopter. That sparked our interest in flight. We followed stories of those who tried to fly.

We decided that the secret to flying was balance. It was like riding a bicycle.

Our first aircraft was made of wood. It was covered with light cloth. The cloth made the wings stronger.

The course of that first flight was crooked because of wind. Well, maybe it was also my lack of experience handling the machine.

9

Make a Balloon Jet Engine

two kitchen chairs

10 feet (3 m) of fishing line or string

drinking straw

balloon

clear tape

helper

 1 Place the two kitchen chairs about 10 feet (3 m) apart. Thread the fishing line or string inside the straw.

2 Tie the fishing line or string between the two chairs. Move the straw to one end.

 3 Blow up the balloon. Instead of tying the end, hold it shut. Have your helper attach the balloon to the straw with a big piece of tape.

4 Release the end of the balloon. What happens?

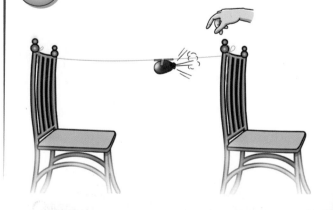

WHO WOULD HAVE THOUGHT?

Jet Airplanes

After the Wright brothers, other inventors took the airplane to new heights. Thirty-six years after Kitty Hawk, the jet airplane was ready. On August 27, 1939, the world's first jet engine started up with a rumble. Within moments, the Heinkel He 178 lifted off from an airfield in Germany.

Jet engines use pressed air mixed with fuel. A jet of hot gases escapes when that mixture catches fire. That produces forward **thrust**. Today, the fastest jet is the Lockheed SR-71A *Blackbird*. The *Blackbird* made its first flight on December 22, 1964. It flies more than 2,200 miles (3,541 km) per hour. That is more than three times the speed of sound.

Jumbo Jet

Cargo Jet

RC 135 Electronic Warfare
Reconnaissance Aircraft

The Bone Crusher

The **internal combustion engine** was invented by Nikolaus August Otto in 1876. That engine paved the way for other inventions, including the motorcycle. In 1885, a German named Gottlieb Daimler built the first motorcycle. Daimler wasn't the only inventor who had thought about building such a machine. Others had tried fitting steam engines to bicycles. Their experiments failed.

Daimler put a gas engine on a bicycle with a wooden frame. The bicycle was known as the "bone crusher." Why? Riding it was rough! Besides adding the motor, Daimler added two small wheels, one on each side. The little wheels helped balance the big wheels. Others before him had tried to make a model with two wheels. Those motorbikes tipped over. Daimler's idea was better. Later on, a two-wheeled motorbike was invented in France. It was called the Millet.

SOMEONE MUST INVENT THE SHOCK ABSORBER!

Meet Gottlieb Daimler

Gottlieb Daimler was born in 1834 near Stuttgart, Germany. His father wanted him to take a job working for the city. Young Gottlieb wouldn't hear of it. He had other interests. He became the first person to put an internal combustion engine on a bike. Afterward, he worked with Wilhelm Maybach to make internal combustion engines more powerful. In time, Daimler became one of the top automobile makers in the world. Daimler didn't invent the internal combustion engine. But he made it better.

The internal combustion engine uses a fuel called gasoline. The engine allows the gasoline to mix with air.

Inside the engine, a spark lights the mixture on fire. *Kaboom!* The gasoline produces an explosion.

If I can harness this power, I can run a bicycle with it. Imagine! Then people wouldn't need to pedal the bike.

I can use heat energy to create mechanical energy. Transportation will change forever.

Roadway Physics

36" x 12" (1 m x 30 cm) piece of smooth plywood or other strong, flat material

several 1-foot (30-cm) sheets of coarse sandpaper

several books

several 3-foot (1-m) sheets of wrinkled printer paper

several 3-foot (1-m) sheets of wax paper

toy car

yardstick or meterstick

notebook and pencil

stopwatch

1 Make a ramp with the books and the plywood. The plywood is your roadway. You can make your roadway more or less slick by covering the surface.

2 Cover the ramp with the sandpaper. Let the car ride down the ramp. Measure how far the car goes past the ramp. Time how long the car runs. Record your observations on paper.

3 Repeat Steps 1 and 2 using wax paper and wrinkled printer paper. Record your observations.

4 Increase or decrease the angle of the ramp by using more or fewer books. Repeat Steps 1 through 3. What conclusions can you draw?

WHO WOULD HAVE THOUGHT?

Motocross Bikes

Once people began riding motorcycles, it didn't take long for the racing to begin! Motorcycle racing took off in the 1920s. That is when British bikers began racing on dirt tracks. Their motorcycles were heavy—some weighed as much as 400 pounds (181 kilograms).

Motorized bikes that run on rough ground are motocross, or MX, bikes. Today's MX bikes are powered by gas. If Neal Saiki gets his way, new MX bikes will run on electricity. Saiki made the Zero X. The bike runs on **lithium** batteries rather than gas. The Zero X weighs about 140 pounds (63.5 kg). When the bike runs out of juice, it needs to be recharged. The bike can travel as far as 40 miles (64 km) between charges. It can go from 0 to 60 miles (97 km) per hour in 4 seconds.

Neal Saiki

On the Road Again

In the late 1800s, early motorcars ran on steam. They were big and clunky. Some looked like sleighs on wheels. Then **engineers** put gasoline engines on their motorcars. One of those engineers was Henry Ford. He built his first "horseless carriage" in 1896. He called it the Quadricycle because it ran on four bicycle tires.

Ford opened a motorcar company in 1903. Car companies then were making only one automobile at a time. It was an expensive way to produce the vehicles. Only rich people could afford them. Ford wanted to make his automobile available to more people. He came up with the idea of the assembly line. Soon he was producing many cars at one time. He called his car the Model T.

The Model T had a plain, simple design. That was another way Ford had been able to cut costs. Almost all of the Model Ts were alike. Ford once said that customers could get the Model T in any color they wanted—as long as it was black.

Meet Henry Ford

Henry Ford could have been a farmer. He was born on a farm near Dearborn, Michigan, in 1863. He hated working in the fields, however. He showed little interest in school, too. He was a poor student. But he liked to work on machinery, especially watches. That tinkering led Henry to build his first automobile. It had an internal combustion engine. Eventually he opened up his own automobile factory. He was able to build his Model Ts at a very affordable price—only $850. His car was easy to use and very sturdy.

THIS IS THE ROAD TO THE FUTURE!

I began using the assembly line in 1913. As ropes pull the frame of a car past a line of workers, each worker adds a part to the car.

The car is finished by the time it reaches the end of the line.

The assembly line cuts the amount of time it takes to make a car from twelve hours to six hours.

I sold 15 million Model Ts in nineteen years!

Build Your Own Horn

35mm film
canister

scissors

straw

balloon

adult helper

1 With the help of an adult, make a hole in the bottom of the film canister with the scissors. Insert the straw in the hole. Make sure the fit is tight.

2 Make another hole in the side of the canister.

3 Cut the balloon as shown. Then cut the top half until it fits over the top of the canister. Stretch the balloon for a tight fit. Put the cap back on the canister over the balloon.

4 Push the straw into the bottom until the straw hits the balloon. Blow into the hole on the side of the canister. If you can't hear anything, move the straw up or down until you do!

WHO WOULD HAVE THOUGHT?

A Flying Car

In the animated TV show *The Jetsons*, George Jetson drives to work in a flying car. If Paul Moller gets his way, all of us might one day fly to our jobs. Moller has invented the world's first flying car—the Skycar.

Moller's $1 million Skycar has eight engines. It has two flight computers. Inside the car's motors are fans. The fans make a strong airflow. That airflow produces enough thrust to lift the 2,400-pound (1,089-kg) vehicle into the air.

The Skycar can travel up to 380 miles (612 km) per hour. The U.S. government must create new rules for flying cars before the Skycar takes to the air!

Blowing Smoke

For thousands of years, people have looked for new ways to power their machines and vehicles. Animals pulled wagons and sleighs. Tall ships caught the wind in huge sails and traveled the oceans. Rushing water powered sawmills.

In 1690 French scientist Denis Papin found a way to use steam as a kind of energy. He built the first steam engine that ran with a **piston**. In 1769 Scottish inventor James Watt constructed the first modern steam engine.

In 1804 Englishman Richard Trevithick took the steam engine and invented the first steam train. Trevithick's train was powerful. It could pull 10 tons (9 tonnes) and seventy people. The first steam engines broke down a lot. Yet, it was less expensive to fix a steam engine than to feed and take care of a team of horses.

Meet Richard Trevithick

Richard Trevithick liked sports. He was born in 1771 in Cornwall, England. He was one of the best wrestlers in the area. When he got older, he worked in the coal mines with his father. He also worked on machines. In 1801 Trevithick built a steam carrier that transported passengers. In 1804 he built the first steam locomotive that ran on rails. The locomotive was so heavy that the rails snapped. Yet that failure did not stop him from working on other steam machines. He made machines for farming. He tried making a machine that could dig tunnels, too.

CAN'T STOP THIS TRAIN!

I use coal or wood to boil water in a boiler. The heat changes that water into steam.

The steam then travels through pipes to the **cylinders**. The cylinders have **valves** that allow the train to go backward and forward.

The cylinders also contain pistons. The steam moves the pistons up and down. Connecting rods drive the train's wheels.

The extra steam and smoke goes out a smokestack.

Stovetop Steam Engine

pot

lid that fits
the pot

water

pinwheel

adult helper

1 Fill a pot with cold water. Put the pot on the stove.

2 Place the blades of the pinwheel over the pot of cold water. Notice that nothing happens to the pinwheel.

3 With an adult's help, start to heat the water. Put the pinwheel over the warming water. Be careful. Hold the pinwheel at the end of the handle. What happens?

4 Put the lid on the pot. Boil the water. Ask your helper to lift the lid. Carefully put the pinwheel over the steam. Fast-moving air molecules create a current!

WHO WOULD HAVE THOUGHT?

Maglev Trains

The *chug, chug, chug* of today's trains is becoming the *whoosh, whoosh, whoosh* of high-speed trains. These superfast machines can travel up to 310 miles (499 km) per hour. They're called maglev trains. *Maglev* is short for "magnetic **levitation.**"

How does a maglev train work? Instead of running on electricity or diesel fuel, it runs on powerful magnets. Magnets move maglev trains at high speeds. The magnets create a powerful **electromagnetic field**. That field moves the train forward.

Instead of riding on the rails, the train is levitated—it rides on a cushion of air. Several companies plan to build maglev systems. Britain made the first maglev train. Shanghai, China, has a big maglev train system.

High–speed train in Shanghai, China

Rocket Science

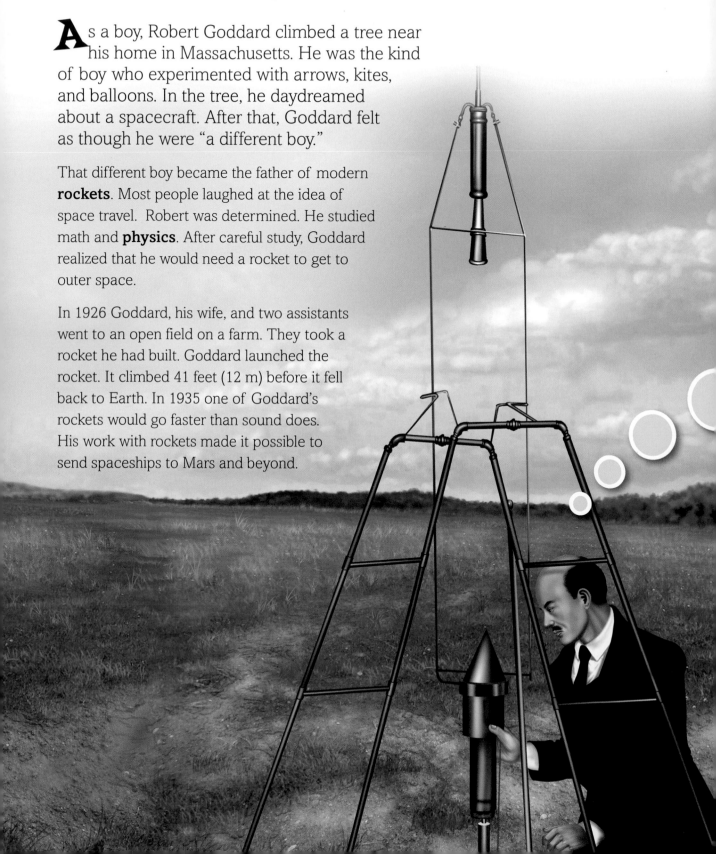

As a boy, Robert Goddard climbed a tree near his home in Massachusetts. He was the kind of boy who experimented with arrows, kites, and balloons. In the tree, he daydreamed about a spacecraft. After that, Goddard felt as though he were "a different boy."

That different boy became the father of modern **rockets**. Most people laughed at the idea of space travel. Robert was determined. He studied math and **physics**. After careful study, Goddard realized that he would need a rocket to get to outer space.

In 1926 Goddard, his wife, and two assistants went to an open field on a farm. They took a rocket he had built. Goddard launched the rocket. It climbed 41 feet (12 m) before it fell back to Earth. In 1935 one of Goddard's rockets would go faster than sound does. His work with rockets made it possible to send spaceships to Mars and beyond.

Meet Robert Goddard

Robert Goddard was born in 1882. He was a fan of the science fiction writer H. G. Wells. Goddard was also a bright boy who read science magazines. He tried many experiments. He even built his own frog city. It had motors and wheels that pumped water into the frogs' "houses." Goddard's first rocket launch in 1926 went unnoticed. But his fourth launch caught the attention of almost everyone. The rocket rose 90 feet (27 m) before crashing. Fire trucks, police, and reporters arrived to see what had happened. After that, Goddard always got noticed!

IF I COULD WALK ON THE MOON . . .

Rockets weigh a lot. The best way to propel a rocket into space may be to divide it into sections.

Each section could carry fuel.

The sections could be fired off in stages. Each one could give the rocket a boost. After firing, each section could drop off.

We can power the rocket with liquid fuel. That would be better than solid fuel, such as the powder used in guns and fireworks. Liquid fuel does not weigh as much.

Rocket Car

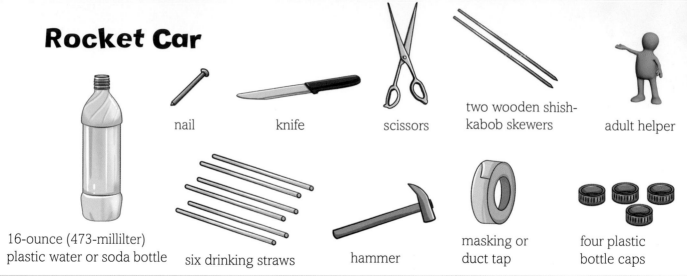

nail

knife

scissors

two wooden shish-kabob skewers

adult helper

16-ounce (473-milliliter)
plastic water or soda bottle

six drinking straws

hammer

masking or
duct tap

four plastic
bottle caps

1 Cut straws (axles) to equal the width of the bottle. Tape as shown. With an adult's help, use the knife to cut the skewers to match the size of the straws. Place the skewers inside the straws. Make a hole in each bottle cap with the nail and hammer. Attach these "wheels" to the skewers.

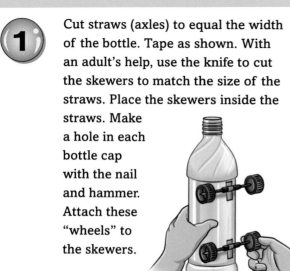

2 Stretch out a balloon. Place its opening over four drinking straws. Tape the opening of the balloon over the opening of the straws. Coil the tape three-quarters of the way down the straws to make a nozzle for the rocket car.

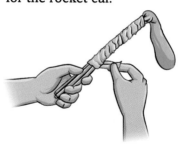

3 Cut an X about 4 inches (10 cm) from the mouth of the bottle. Put the nozzle through the X and thread it through the mouth of the bottle. Leave about an inch (2.5 cm) of the nozzle hanging from the mouth of the bottle. Seal the X opening with the tape.

4 Put your car on the floor. Blow into the nozzle until the balloon is filled. Put your finger over the nozzle's opening. When ready, remove your finger and watch the car rocket across the floor!

WHO WOULD HAVE THOUGHT?

Rocket Plane

Rockets have come a long way since Robert Goddard sent up his first liquid-fuel rocket. In fact, passengers will soon fly easily into outer space. A number of companies are building a new type of vehicle. It is part plane and part rocket. It will take people just above Earth's atmosphere.

Companies with names such as XCOR Aerospace are working overtime to make the rocket plane. XCOR has designed a rocket plane called *Lynx*. It is about the size of a small plane. The people at XCOR are hoping *Lynx* will have its first voyage in 2010. It will be able to fly into space several times a day.

XCOR Rocket Vehicle

Timeline

The Mesopotamians invent the oldest known wheel.

3000 B.C.
The chariot makes its debut.

600 B.C.
The Phoenicians fashion a reed sail and navigate around the southern tip of Africa.

1690
French scientist Denis Papin invents the steam engine.

1783
The Montgolfier brothers launch a hot-air balloon in Paris.

1804
Richard Trevithick invents the world's first steam locomotive.

1885
Gottlieb Daimler builds a motorcycle.

2002

The commercial maglev train goes into service in Shanghai, China.

1969

Two Americans land on the Moon.

1926

A rocket invented by Robert Goddard successfully flies.

1913

Henry Ford puts the first assembly line to use.

1903

Orville and Wilbur Wright fly the first motor-powered airplane.

Glossary

aeronautics the science of flight.

cylinder a solid or hollow object that is shaped like a drum or a soup can.

electromagnetic field an area that is magnetized by electricity, which is electrons in movement.

engineer a person trained in engineering. An engineer may design bridges, airplanes, and roads.

experiment to make a practical test in order to prove or disprove a theory.

glider an aircraft that flies without a motor. Rising air currents keep it in the air.

helium an odorless, colorless gas that is the second most plentiful element in the universe.

hydrogen a gas that has no color, odor, or taste and is the most plentiful element in the universe.

internal combustion engine an engine powered by small, controlled explosions.

levitation the act of rising into the air.

lift the force that causes a vehicle to rise in the air.

lithium a soft, silver-white element that is the lightest of all metals.

physics the science that deals with matter and energy and the laws governing them.

piston the part that fits tightly in an engine cylinder and, when it moves, moves a rod.

rocket a device projected into the air by a flow of hot gases released when a special fuel mix explodes.

thrust a sudden, strong drive or push.

valve piece in a pipe that moves, changing the flow of liquid or gas through the pipe.

To L arn Mor

Books

First Flight: The Story of the Wright Brothers by Caryn Jenner. Dorling Kindersley Publishing, 2003.

Henry Ford: Putting the World on Wheels by Time for Kids Editors. HarperCollins Publishers, 2008.

Rocket Man: The Story of Robert Goddard by Thomas Streissguth. Lerner Publishing Group, 1995.

Websites

Courtesy of the Smithsonian Institution, *America on the Move* is a website exploring the history of transportation in America. **http://americanhistory.si.edu/onthemove/**

History.com traces the fascinating history of cars and the automobile industry. **http://www.history.com/encyclopedia.do?articleId=201868**

The National Air and Space Museum outlines the history of flight, from Kitty Hawk to the latest mission to Mars, in this online exhibit. **http://www.nasm.si.edu/**

Index